SQUIGGLING
ANIMALS

Squiggling - Animals

ISBN: 978-87-974087-4-2

Authors: Sanne Lausen Wolff & Janni Lausen Wolff
Illustrations: Sanne Lausen Wolff

Layout: Sanne Lausen Wolff & Janni Lausen Wolff

First edition, First printing 2023

ABOUT US

Farveskyen is a publishing house and an online forum focused on creativity in children and adults.

Drawing enhances the ability to immerse oneself, concentrate, and problem-solve, and it serves as an outlet for imagination. Once the techniques are learned, one can create anything using a pencil.

Anyone can put a pencil to paper and create a squiggle, just as anyone can produce sound from an instrument. However, making the instrument produce a melody is not the same as being able to play it. Just as playing an instrument, drawing is a discipline that requires learning and practice.

With Farveskyen's guides, everyone can draw. We love drawings, even those that are not perfect or that turned out completely different than imagined. We help you develop the technical skills you need to one day transfer all your own ideas onto paper.

TO ALL CHILDREN WHO LOVE TO DRAW AND ALL ADULTS WHO NEVER REALLY LEARNED.

A BIG THANK YOU TO EVERYONE WHO TRIED OUR DRAWING GUIDES AND CONTRIBUTED THEIR BEAUTIFUL DRAWINGS TO THE BOOK - AND A VERY SPECIAL GREETING TO CAROLINE, DAGMAR, FENJA, HOLGER, LUCA, ASGER, AND THØGER, WHO INSPIRE US EVERY SINGLE DAY AND FILL OUR WORLD WITH COLORS.

SANNE LAUSEN WOLFF & JANNI LAUSEN WOLFF

SQUIGGLING ANIMALS

Content

Boring adult talk

Welcome to the first book in our series of drawing guides - ”Squiggling”.

A squiggle is a wavy or curvy line, often drawn in a playful or spontaneous manner, and squiggling is the first kind of drawing any os us do. We chose to name this series ”Squiggling” because the book teaches the reader how to tame their squiggles to construct drawings and it emphasizes the importance of thinking like an artist along the way.

The drawings in the book are simple, and the instructions are easy to follow with minimal changes from step to step. The book can be used by anyone, from brand-new budding artists as young as five years old to adults seeking practice or inspiration.

The book contains step-by-step drawing guides, and the illustrations can be used even without the written instructions. However, occasionally the drawings are supplemented with a brief explanation or a tip to help you understand why your lines should look as instructed.

If you are an adult who purchased the book to help your child develop their drawing skills, you can assist your child by completing one or more of the drawings side by side with them to introduce them to the method.

Tips for your drawing

1. Draw big. Many people who follow step-by-step guides tend to reproduce the illustrations in the same size as they appear in the book. While you should mimic the shapes in the book, feel free to make them larger.
2. Draw in the middle of the paper to minimize the risk of running out of space.
3. Sketch lightly - meaning draw without pressing the pencil against the paper.
4. Move your hand over the paper multiple times until the stroke is exactly as you want it to be
5. Draw curves, not straight lines. Even lines that appear straight in nature come to life when you allow them to curve slightly in your drawing.
6. Save your drawings. It's fun to track your own progress, so save your drawings, even if they may not be perfect at first.
7. Don't be a perfectionist. Enjoy the things that hit the mark and learn to appreciate the small mistakes.
8. The best advice we can give to those who want to become really skilled at drawing is: Draw! No one is born as a talented artist. Everyone who can draw has practiced. So, the best thing you can do to become good at drawing is to draw.

What do you need?

Drawing doesn't require a lot of equipment.
All the illustrations in this book are designed to be reproduced using just paper, a pencil, and an eraser.
That being said, here are a few tips for your drawing tools and how to use them:

Use a blue colored pencil

A little trick that many artists use is to sketch the initial draft with a blue colored pencil. After that, the outlines are drawn with a regular pencil or possibly a black marker.
This way, the initial sketch appears almost invisible, and it doesn't matter if incorrect lines are drawn during the process.

THERE MAY BE PLENTY OF MISTAKES IN THE FINAL SKETCH, BUT THAT'S OKAY. THE BLUE LINES WILL ONLY BE FAINTLY VISIBLE WHEN THE OUTLINE IS DRAWN WITH BLACK.

Colored pencils or markers

Whether you want to color your drawings is up to you. This book primarily aims to teach you to observe and reproduce simple shapes, and you may stick to drawing the line drawings. However, if you want to color the drawings, colored pencils or alcohol-based markers are good tools for this. Colored pencils are easy to use and inexpensive to acquire, and quality pencils can provide a really nice color result. Alcohol-based markers quickly provide vibrant and clear colors, and the markers can be layered on top of each other to create smooth color transitions.

Fineliner

Once your sketch is complete, you can draw the outer lines (contours) with a darker color. You can certainly use a regular pencil, but the best result is achieved with a small fine-tip black marker called a fineliner. Fineliners are available in different sizes, and the size you should use depends on the scale of your drawings.

THE HEDGEHOG HERE HAS BEEN COLORED USING ALCOHOL-BASED MARKERS.

Colors, light and shadow

Flat colors

Coloring is for most people one of the first drawing skills we learn. We have all used coloring books and practiced coloring each section in a single color. This is called "flat colors" and is used in contrast to coloring with depth (indicating light and shadow).

It is perfectly fine to color the animals in this book with flat colors. However, you can also choose to experiment with light and shadow.

1.

DRAW A LINE DRAWING BY FOLLOWING THE BOOK'S DRAWING GUIDES UP TO THE LAST STEP BEFORE COLORING - HERE, WE'LL USE THE BUNNY AS AN EXAMPLE.

2.

DETERMINE WHICH BASE COLOR THE DRAWING SHOULD HAVE AND COLOR THE PARTS THAT SHOULD HAVE THAT COLOR.

3.

ADD COLOR TO THE REMAINING AREAS. CONSIDER WHETHER THEY SHOULD BE DARKER OR LIGHTER THAN THE BASE COLOR. INSIDE THE EARS, THERE IS NO LIGHT, SO A DARKER COLOR IS CHOSEN HERE. YOU CAN ALSO ADD COLOR OUTSIDE THE LINES, LIKE HERE, WHERE THE BUNNY'S CHEEKS ARE COLORED PINK.

Light and shadow

Light and shadow can be challenging to master, but you can actually go a long way with two very simplified rules:

1. Light falls on the surfaces facing towards the sun.

2. Shadow falls on the surfaces that sunlight cannot reach

1\.

THE SUNLIGHT COMES FROM ABOVE AND HITS THE SURFACES THAT ARE FACING UPWARD (AND A BIT ON THE SIDES). THERE WILL ALSO ALWAYS BE LIGHT REFLECTING IN THE EYES.

YOU CAN'T APPLY A LIGHT COLOR ON TOP OF A DARK ONE, SO FIRST DECIDE WHICH AREAS SHOULD BE THE BRIGHTEST AND COLOR THEM WITH A COMPLETELY LIGHT SHADE OR HIGHLIGHT THEM WITH WHITE.

" EYES ARE LOCATED INSIDE THE EYE SOCKETS, WHICH IS WHY THERE IS ALWAYS A DARKER AREA AROUND THE EYES.

2\.

NEXT, APPLY THE BASE COLORS AROUND THE LIGHT AREAS. THIS RABBIT HAS ONLY ONE BASE COLOR, BUT BE CAREFUL TO USE THE CORRECT COLOR IN EACH AREA IF YOUR ANIMAL IS MULTICOLORED.

3\.

FINALLY, ADD A DARKER SHADE TO THE SURFACES THAT ARE FACING DOWNWARD OR ARE HIDDEN BENEATH OR BEHIND SOMETHING.

Animals in the forest

Fiona the Fox

What makes this fox look like a fox, especially, are its wide, pointed ears and its large, bushy tail. And though the drawing is cute, even without colors or in other colors, a red or orange fur would make it clear that it is indeed a fox you have drawn.

1.

START WITH A MUSHROOM-LIKE SHAPE.

2.

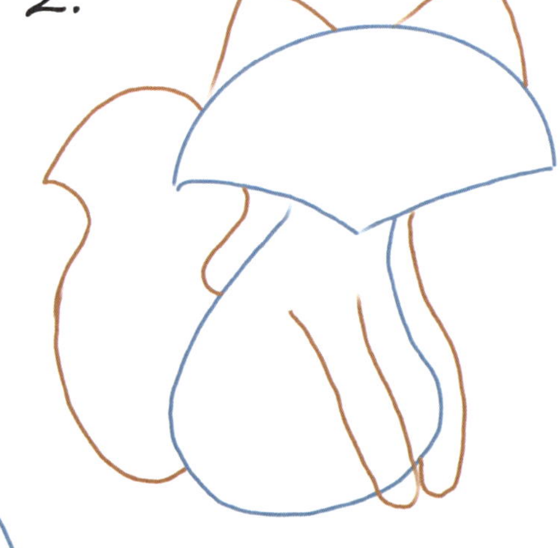

A CURVED S-SHAPED LINE MAKES THE TAIL LOOK SOFT.

3.

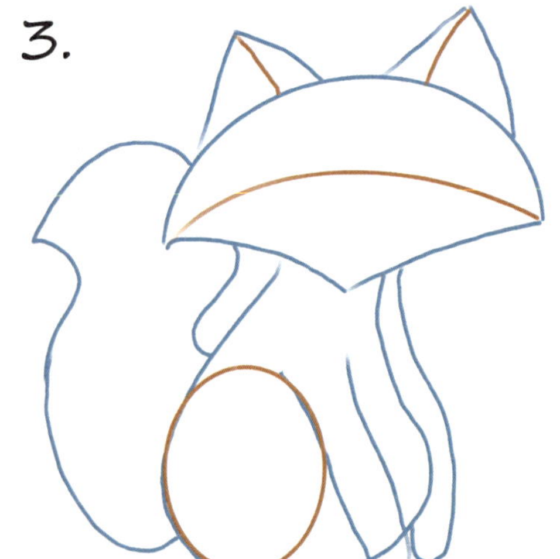

THE FOX'S EYES ARE SMALL AND SPACED FAR APART.

4.

5.

DRAW A JAGGED LINE ACROSS THE FOX'S TAIL AND LEGS TO INDICATE FUR.

THE WHITE DOTS IN THE EYES ARE THE LIGHT REFLECTING - TRY LOOKING AT YOUR OWN EYES IN THE MIRROR. YOU WILL ALWAYS BE ABLE TO SEE SUCH A REFLECTION.

6.

> DRAW THE OUTLINES WITH BLACK. ERASE OR OMIT DRAWING WHERE THE LINES ARE MARKED WITH YELLOW.

Betty the Bat

The bat is characterized by its small body, large ears, and jagged wings.

1.

2.

THE BAT'S EARS ARE DRAWN AS A SOFT V-SHAPE FROM THE MIDDLE OF THE HEAD DOWN TO THE JAW.

3.

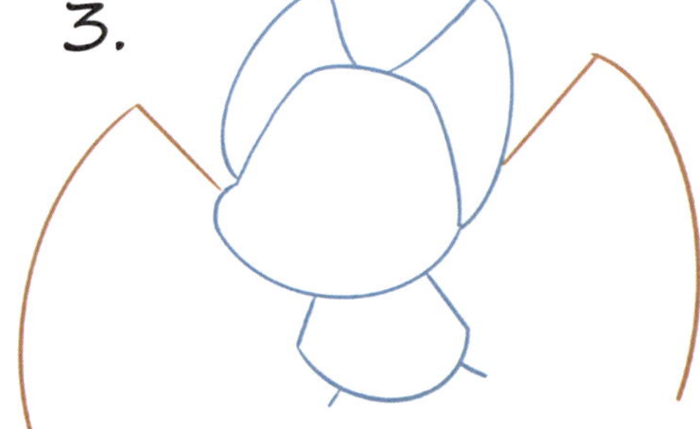

THE WINGS ARE WIDE AND AS TALL AS THE BAT.

4.

5.

THE MOUTH IS WIDE WITH SMALL, POINTED TEETH.

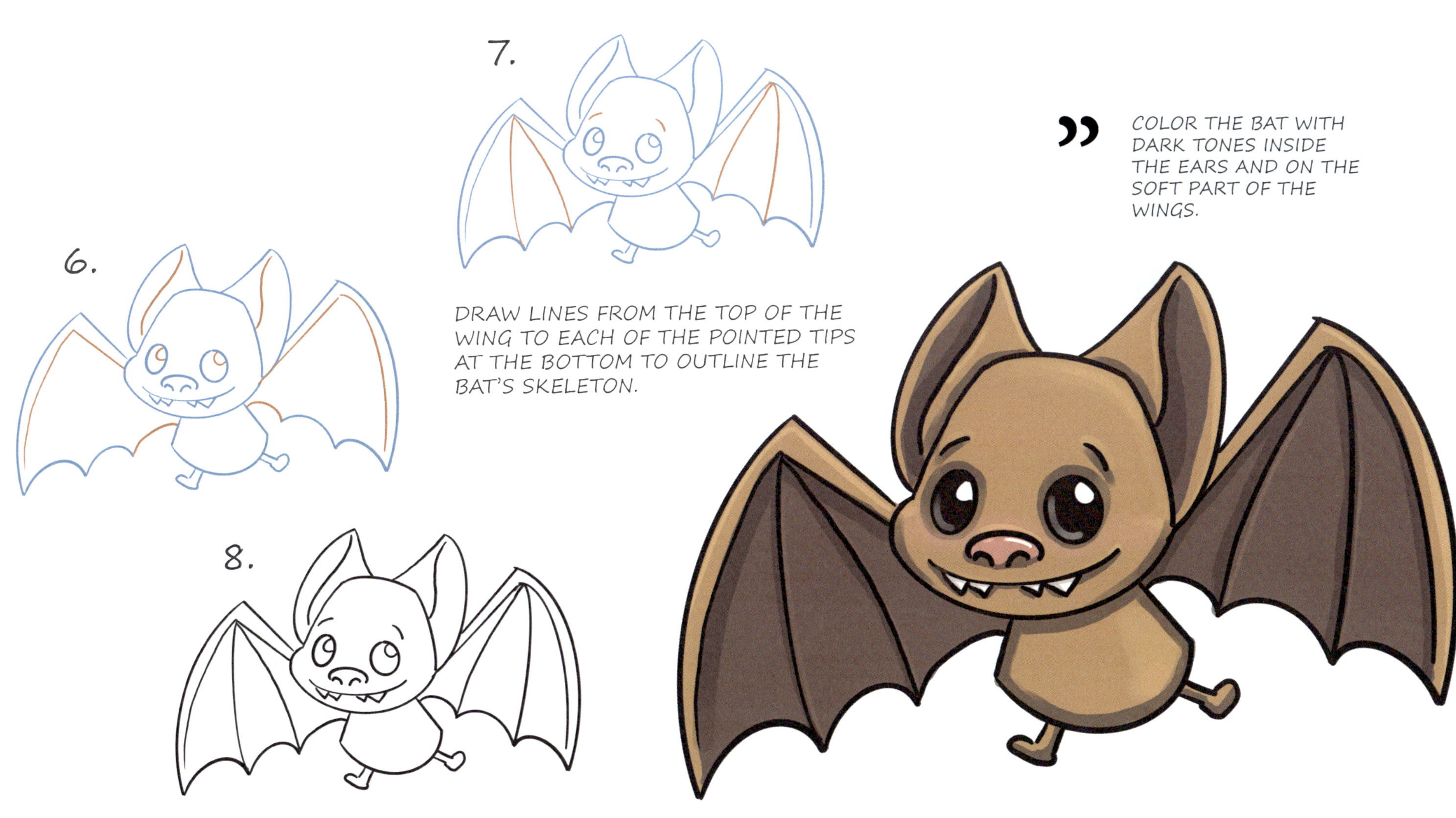

DRAW LINES FROM THE TOP OF THE WING TO EACH OF THE POINTED TIPS AT THE BOTTOM TO OUTLINE THE BAT'S SKELETON.

COLOR THE BAT WITH DARK TONES INSIDE THE EARS AND ON THE SOFT PART OF THE WINGS.

Doris the Deer

The deer is characterized by its large eyes, small antlers, and spots on its rump.

1.

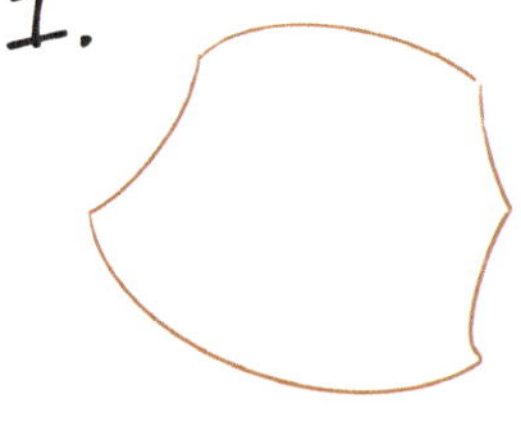

THE LOWER PART OF THE ROE DEER'S HEAD IS THE WIDEST. IT SHOULD BE SLIGHTLY CURVED AND SLOPE DOWN TOWARDS THE RIGHT.

2.

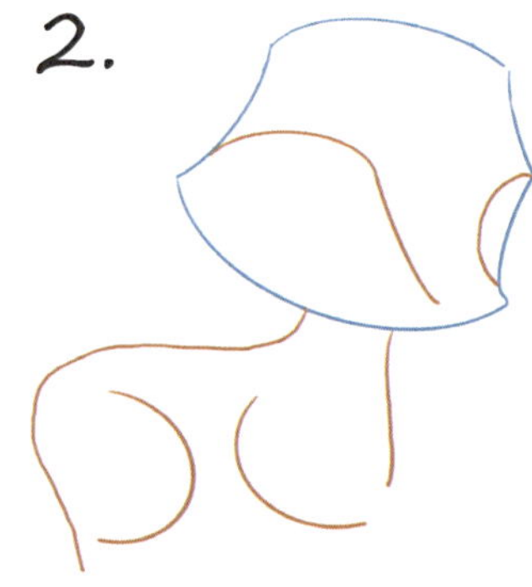

3.

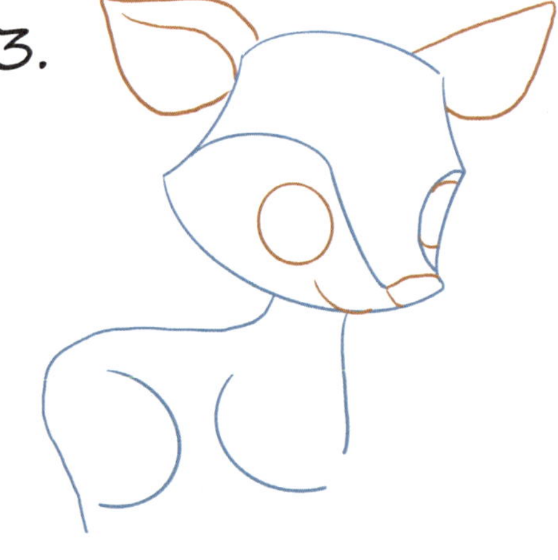

4.

THE ANTLERS ON THE RIGHT SIDE OF THE DEER ARE ONLY DRAWN FROM THE TOP OF THE HEAD, AS THEY ARE MEANT TO APPEAR ATTACHED TO A PART OF THE HEAD THAT IS NOT VISIBLE.

5.

6.

COLOR THE DEER WITH A LIGHT TONE ON THE CHEST AND THE LOWER PART OF THE HEAD, AND A DARKER TONE ON THE BODY AND THE UPPER PART OF THE HEAD.

Scarlett the Squirrel

The most characteristic features of a squirrel are its large, bushy tail and its pointed, long-haired ears. The round and soft shapes make the squirrel look cute.

1.

THE HEAD OF THE SQUIRREL IS A CIRCLE, AND THE BODY IS PEAR-SHAPED.

2.

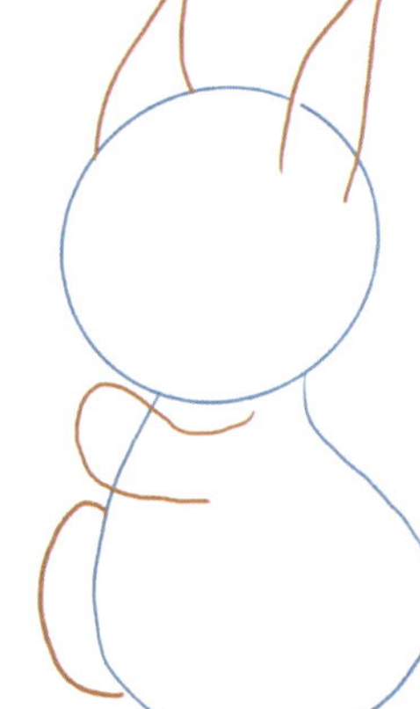

3.

DRAW THE LARGE TAIL IN TWO PARTS; A SEMICIRCLE EXTENDING FROM THE UPPER PART OF THE SQUIRREL'S HEAD AND THEN AN S-SHAPE FROM THE SQUIRREL'S RUMP.

4.

THE SQUIRREL'S EYES ARE TWO LARGE OVALS. THE FARTHEST EYE SHOULD BE SLIGHTLY SMALLER THAN THE NEAREST ONE TO INDICATE PERSPECTIVE AND DEPTH.

5.

DRAW THE LEFT THIGH AS A CIRCLE THAT FOLLOWS THE LOWER PART OF THE SQUIRREL'S BODY.

6.

COLOR THE SQUIRREL IN TWO COLORS. USE THE LIGHTEST ONE ON THE SNOUT AREA AND THE BELLY.

Beatrice the Badger

The badger has a flat, stout body, a pointed snout, and small ears. And of course it has the distinctive stripes across its head.

1.

DRAW THE BADGER'S SNOUT AS A SOFT V-SHAPE. THE BACK OF THE HEAD IS A SEMICIRCLE FROM ONE SIDE OF THE V TO THE OTHER.

2.

THE BODY IS A LARGE, FLAT OVAL.

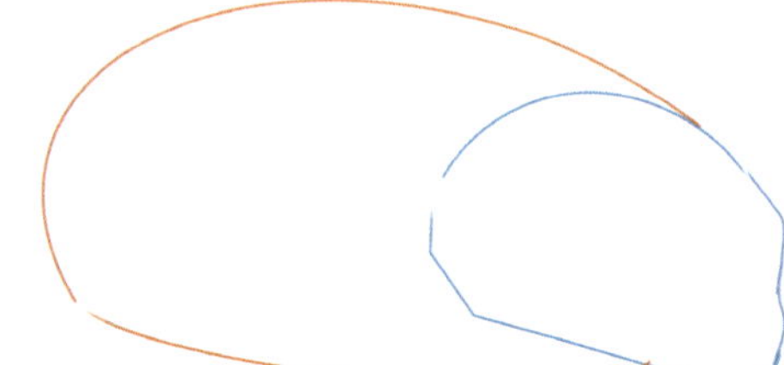

3.

4.

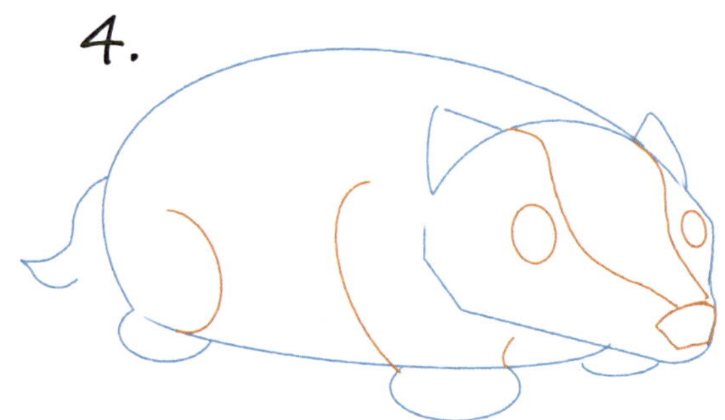

5.

THE STRIPES ARE DRAWN AS A FLAT S-SHAPE TO ACHIEVE DEPTH.

6.

DRAW JAGGED LINES ON THE BODY AND TAIL OF THE BADGER, AS WELL AS ON THE TOP OF ITS PAWS, TO INDICATE A SCRUFFY FUR.

7.

AT FIRST GLANCE, THE BADGER APPEARS TO BE WHITE, GRAY, AND BLACK. HOWEVER, IN REALITY, THREE DIFFERENT SHADES OF GRAY ARE USED. TRUE BLACK IS RARELY FOUND IN NATURE AND THEREFORE SHOULD BE SELDOM USED IN COLORING.

Children and parents draw Animals in the Forest

THØGER'S MOM 37 YEARS

THØGER 5 YEARS

HOLGER 7 YEARS

ASGER 5 YEARS

GRY 14 YEARS

Animals in the garden

Hedvig the Hedgehog

The hedgehog is a small ball with a flat bottom. Its back is covered in spines, and only a small, cute face peeks out from underneath them.

1.

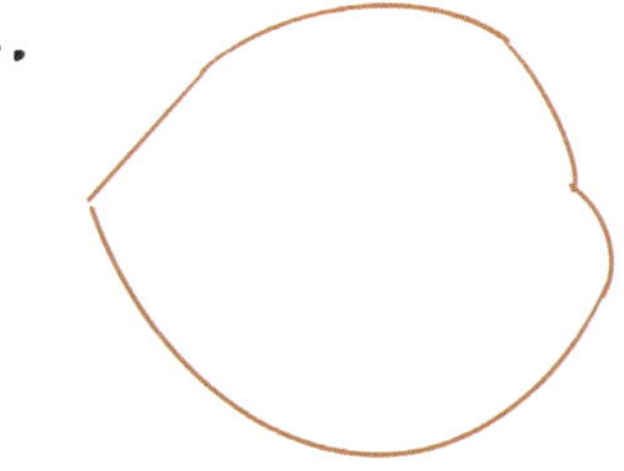

THE HEDGEHOG'S CHEEK PROTRUDES ON THE LEFT SIDE OF ITS HEAD BECAUSE WE ARE VIEWING THE HEAD AT AN ANGLE FROM THE SIDE.

2.

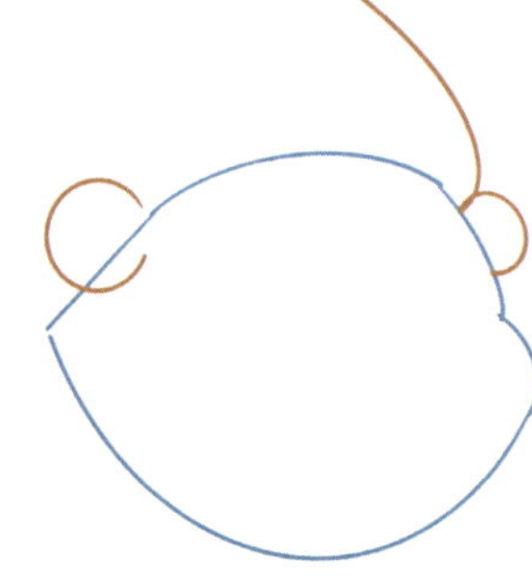

STORE ZIGZAG-KURVER HENOVER RYGGEN MARKERER PINDSVINETS PIGGE.

3.

4.

THE LEFT EYE IS A SEMICIRCLE RIGHT UP AGAINST THE EDGE OF THE FACE, WHILE THE RIGHT EYE IS APPROXIMATELY TWICE AS LARGE. THE CURVE AT THE BOTTOM INDICATES A SMALL, CHUBBY CHEEK.

5\.

DRAW TWO CURVES OVER EACH OF THE HEDGEHOG'S PAWS TO INDICATE THE TOES.

6\.

A LITTLE PINK COLOR OVER THE CHEEK AND SNOUT MAKES THE HEDGEHOG EXTRA CUTE.

Cameron the Caterpillar

The shape of the caterpillar should be soft and flexible. Large eyes and antennae give the drawing character.

1.

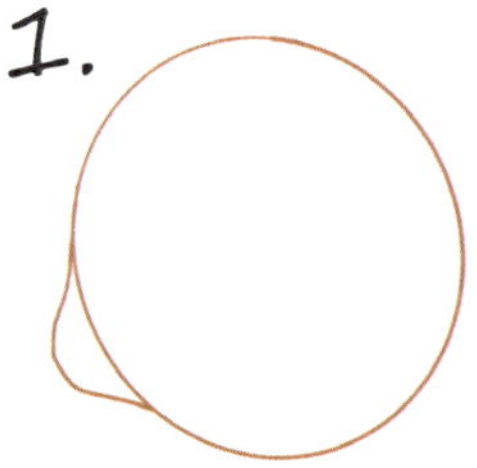

2.

DRAW A SERIES OF SEMICIRCLES EXTENDING FROM THE HEAD - THE SEMICIRCLES SHOULD BECOME SMALLER THE FURTHER THEY ARE FROM THE HEAD.

3.

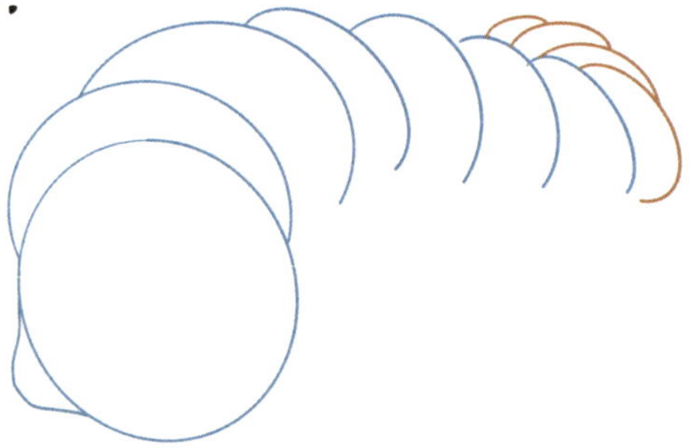

LET THE LAST SEGMENTS OF THE CATERPILLAR OVERLAP THE OTHERS, FORMING SMALL BUMPS. THIS MARKS A BEND IN THE BODY.

4.

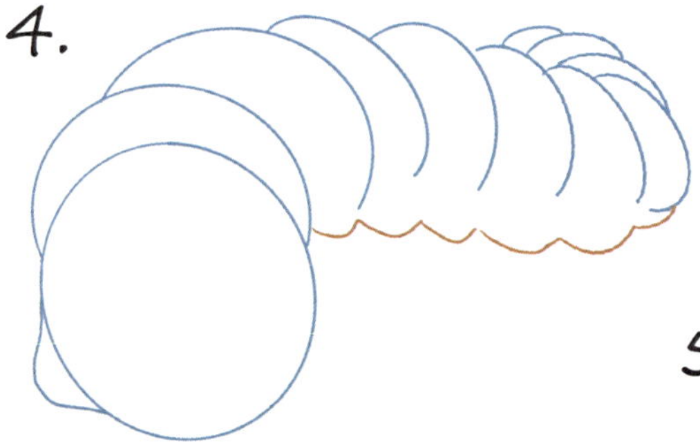

5.

ADD SMALL LEGS ALL ALONG THE UNDERSIDE OF THE BODY, AND GIVE YOUR CATERPILLAR A FACE AND ANTENNAE.

6.

LET ONE LEG PROTRUDE BEHIND THE FRONT LEG ON THE RIGHT SIDE OF THE CATERPILLAR.

7.

" THIS CATERPILLAR IS GREEN, BUT YOU CAN USE ANY COLOR YOU LIKE.

Bonnie the Blue Tit

The blue tit is a small, chubby bird with thin legs and long toes. What sets the blue tit apart from most other birds is the color pattern on its head and body.

1.

ONE SIDE OF THE BODY SHAPE IS LEFT OPEN TO MAKE ROOM FOR THE WING.

2.

3.

MARK THE BORDER BETWEEN THE HEAD AND BODY. BY ALLOWING THE LINE TO CURVE DOWNWARD, YOU CREATE A SENSE OF DEPTH IN THE FIGURE.

4.

5.

THE BLUE TIT'S WING IS TRICOLORED. BY MARKING THE TRANSITION BETWEEN THE COLORS WITH A WAVY LINE, YOU CREATE A SIMPLE SUGGESTION OF FEATHERS OVERLAPPING EACH OTHER.

" YOUR DRAWING IS UNDOUBTEDLY A NICE BIRD AS IT IS NOW. BUT IT BECOMES A TRUE BLUE TIT WHEN YOU ADD THE YELLOW, BLUE, AND GREEN COLORS.

Morgan the Mole

The mole is known for being blind, so it has closed eyes. Its front paws are small shovels with wide claws, and its snout is long and snout-like.

1.

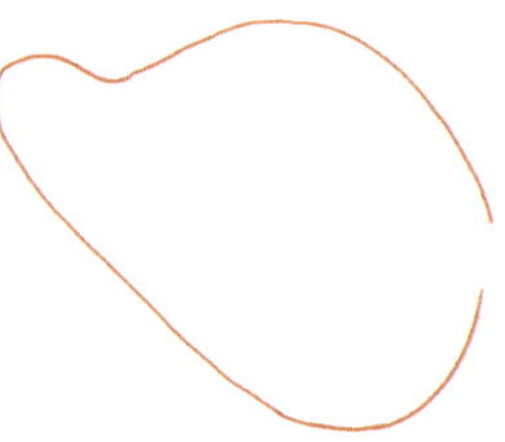

2.

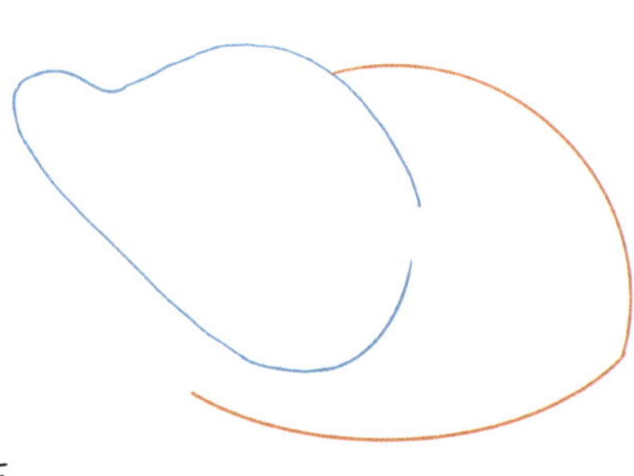

3.

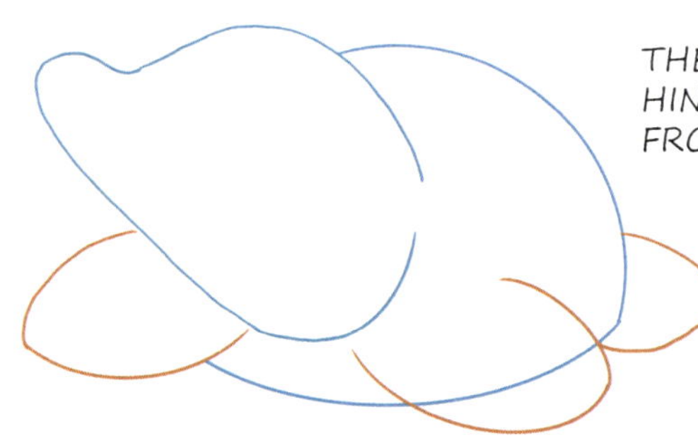

THE LEGS ARE DRAWN AS C-SHAPES. THE HIND LEG SHOULD BE SMALLER THAN THE FRONT LEGS.

4.

GIVE THE MOLE A HAPPY, WIDE MOUTH.

5.

DRAW A SMALL SQUARE BELOW THE MOUTH TO GIVE THE MOLE TEETH.

6.

CREATE A U-SHAPE UNDER THE MOUTH TO DRAW AN OPEN AND VERY HAPPY MOUTH.

7.

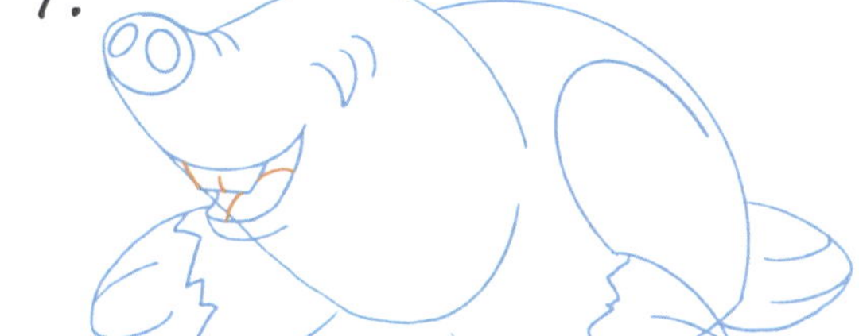

DRAW A TONGUE AND A SMALL GAP BETWEEN THE FRONT TEETH.

8.

" THE MOLE HERE IS PURPLE. OF COURSE, MOLES ARE NOT PURPLE IN REALITY, BUT ADDING SOME COLOR CAN MAKE YOUR DRAWING A BIT MORE CARTOON-LIKE.

Sonia the Snail

A snail is soft. It doesn't have a skeleton, so it can bend and stretch in all directions. There are snails without shells, but the snail shell is still the most characteristic feature of a snail, so Sonia here has a beautiful shell on her back.

1.

2.

3.

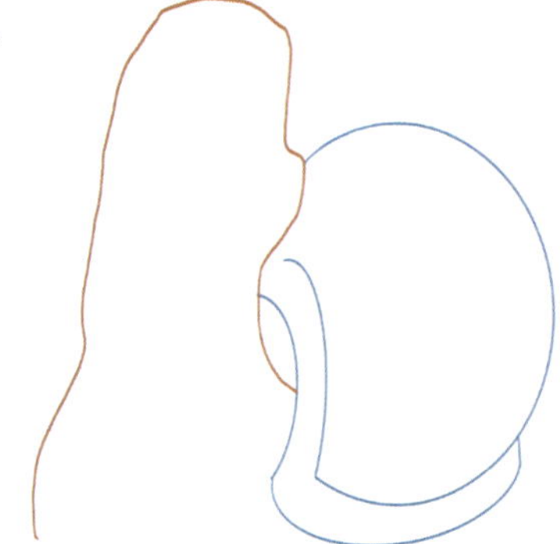

THE SNAIL'S BODY CAN HAVE A SLIGHTLY WAVY LINE. THE CHEEK BULGES OUT ON THE LEFT SIDE OF THE SNAIL.

4.

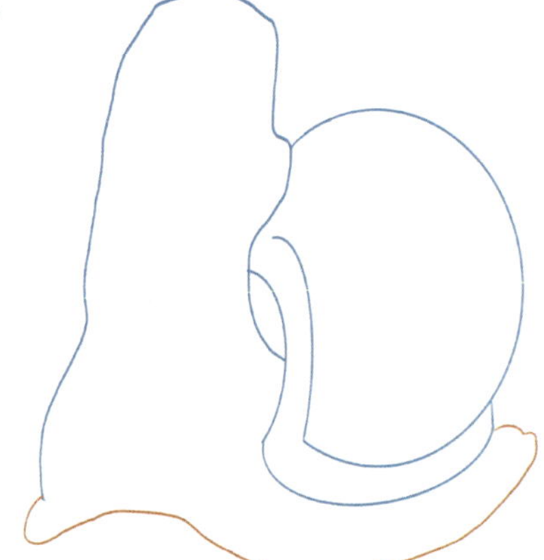

THE SNAIL'S UNDERSIDE SHOULD BE SOFT AND FLEXIBLE. THIS IS ILLUSTRATED BY AN S-SHAPED CURVE AT THE BOTTOM.

5.

PLACE THE MOUTH AND EYES SLIGHTLY ASKEW.

6.

7.

THE STRIPES ON THE SNAIL SHELL ARE CURVES THAT FOLLOW THE SHAPE OF THE SHELL AND CREATE DEPTH.

8.

BE CAREFUL WHEN OUTLINING THE DOTS. THEY SHOULD GIVE THE SNAIL'S SURFACE SOME TEXTURE, BUT THEY SHOULDN'T BE BLACK SPOTS.

” YOUR SNAIL CAN HAVE ANY COLORS YOU LIKE, BUT MAKE THE INSIDE OF THE SNAIL'S SHELL DARKER THAN THE REST. INSIDE THE SHELL, THERE IS NO LIGHT, SO IT SHOULD APPEAR DARKER.

Children and parents draw animals in the garden

HOLGER'S DAD 39 YEARS
GRY 14 YEARS
GRY 14 YEARS
FENJA 14 YEARS
ASGER 5 YEARS

Animals in the home

Brenda the Bunny

The bunny has a small body with large hind legs and big feet. It is often depicted with visible front teeth, and of course, it has long ears.

1.

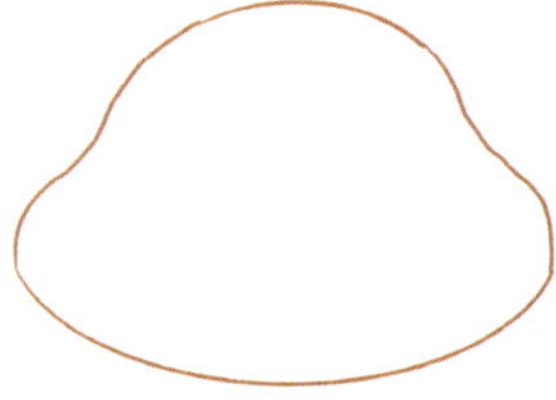

THE BUNNY HAS SMALL CHUBBY CHEEKS, WHICH MEANS THAT THE WIDTH OF ITS HEAD IS APPROXIMATELY ONE AND A HALF TIMES ITS HEIGHT.

2.

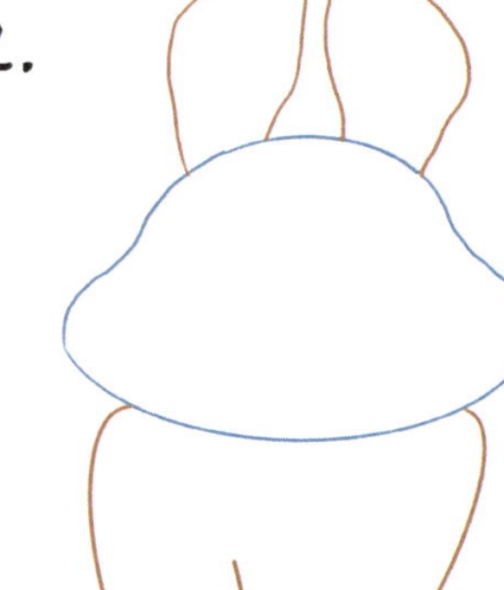

3.

4.

THE BUNNY'S FORMS ARE ROUND AND SOFT. THEREFORE, YOU SHOULD USE C AND U SHAPES FOR ALMOST ALL PARTS OF THE DRAWING.

5.
CREATE A FLUFFY FUR ON THE BUNNY'S
CHEST BY DRAWING A JAGGED
BOUNDARY THAT OVERLAPS THE FRONT
LEGS.
6.
GIVE YOUR BUNNY A
PINK TONE ON ITS NOSE
AND CHEEKS.

Hugo the Hamster

A hamster is a small round ball with big cheeks, visible incisors, and whiskers.

1.

HUGO HERE IS SEEN FROM A LEFT ANGLE, SO THE CHEEK BULGES OUT ON THE HAMSTER'S RIGHT SIDE.

2.

THE EARS ARE QUITE LARGE BUT LIE ALMOST FLAT AGAINST THE HEAD.

3.

DRAW THE FORELEGS AS TWO CIRCLES THAT ALMOST MEET AT THE TOP OF THE HAMSTER'S CHEST.

4.

5\.

DRAW THE FUR AS SMALL SPIKES ALL AROUND THE HAMSTER'S BODY.

6\.

"

HUGO HERE IS A GOLDEN HAMSTER, SO HE IS COLORED IN LIGHT BROWN TONES. SHOULD YOURS BE THE SAME?

Clara the Cat

The cat is primarily recognized for its slim and elegant body. In this illustrated version of a cat, it is more compact and has a large head to make it look extra cute.

1.

2. THE CAT ARCHES ITS BACK AND PUSHES ITS CHEST FORWARD. THE ARCH IN THE BACK IS ACHIEVED BY DRAWING AN S-SHAPE FROM THE NECK DOWN TO THE CAT'S LEFT HIND LEG.

3.

4.

A LINE FROM THE TIP OF THE EAR DOWN TO THE CAT'S HEAD INDICATES A FOLD ON THE EAR AND CREATES DEPTH.

CHOOSE THREE BEAUTIFUL COLORS FOR YOUR CAT. USE ONE FOR THE LOWER PART OF THE FACE, ANOTHER FOR THE UPPER PART, AND THE LAST ONE FOR THE FUR ON THE OUTER PART OF THE TAIL, THE TOP OF THE HEAD, AND THE CHEST.

Molly the Mouse

The mouse is small and round. It has large ears and eyes, and the tail is long and thin.

1.

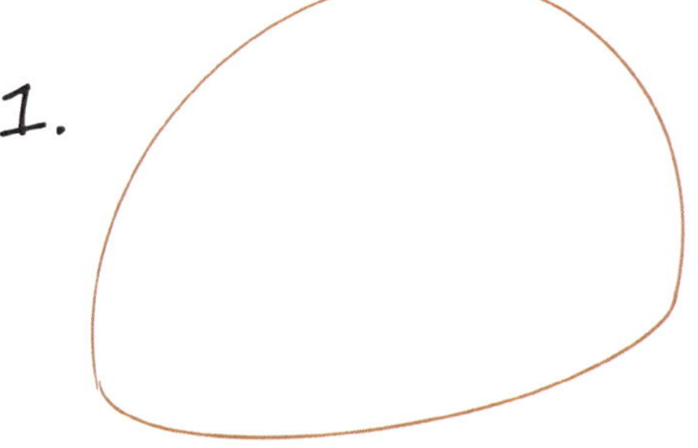

THE HEAD AND BODY OF THE MOUSE ARE ONE UNIFIED SHAPE.

2.

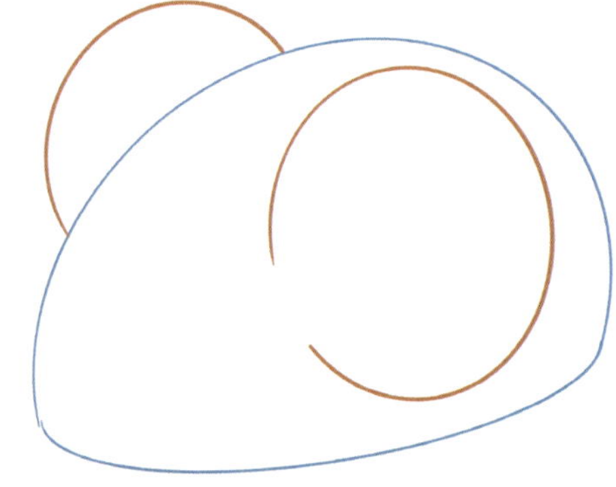

THERE IS AN OPENING ON THE SIDE OF THE EAR THAT CONNECTS THE EAR TO THE BODY. THE RIGHT EAR IS HIDDEN BEHIND THE BODY AND SHOULD THEREFORE BE DRAWN ONLY AS THE TOP PART OF A CIRCLE.

3.

REMEMBER TO DRAW THE EYE FARTHEST AWAY SMALLER THAN THE CLOSEST ONE.

4.

MOLLY HERE IS GRAY, BUT PERHAPS YOUR MOUSE COULD HAVE A DIFFERENT COLOR - MAYBE BROWN? OR HOW ABOUT PURPLE?

Charlie the Chihuahua

Chihuahuas are small dogs with distinctively large eyes. They can have different appearances, but Charlie here has long-haired ears and a large, fluffy tail.

1.

THE HEAD OF A CHIHUAHUA IS ACTUALLY A SQUARE, BUT WITH SIDES THAT CURVE OUTWARD.

2.

3.

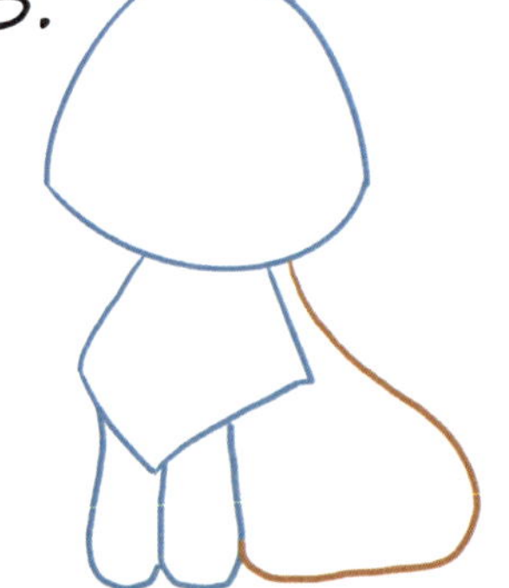

DRAW AN S-SHAPED CURVE FROM THE NECK TO THE RUMP AND HIND LEG.

4.

5.

LARGE TUFTS WITH POINTED ENDS POINTING DOWNWARD MAKE THE EARS FLUFFY AND LONG-HAIRED.

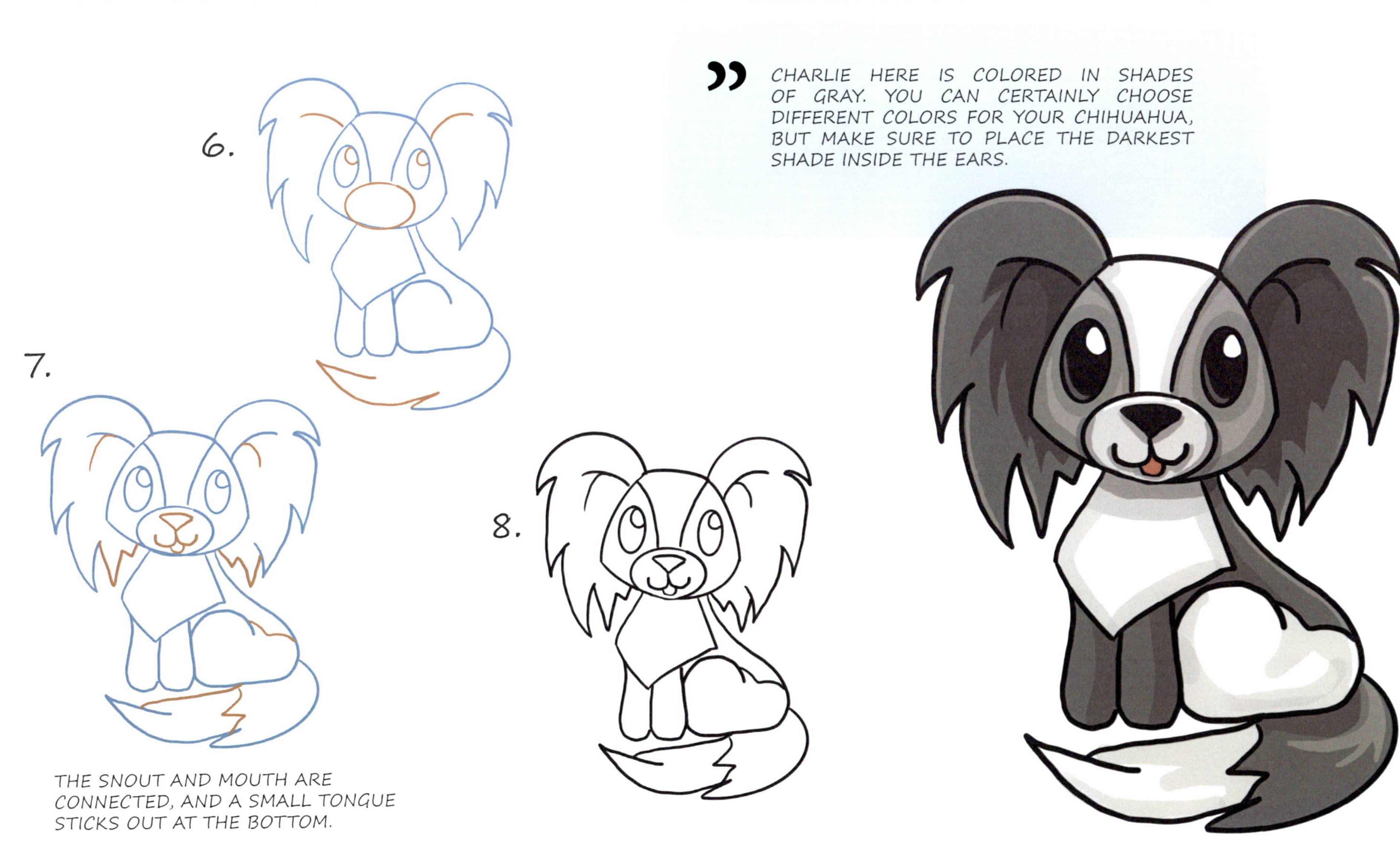

THE SNOUT AND MOUTH ARE CONNECTED, AND A SMALL TONGUE STICKS OUT AT THE BOTTOM.

CHARLIE HERE IS COLORED IN SHADES OF GRAY. YOU CAN CERTAINLY CHOOSE DIFFERENT COLORS FOR YOUR CHIHUAHUA, BUT MAKE SURE TO PLACE THE DARKEST SHADE INSIDE THE EARS.

Children and parents draw animals in the home

SVEA 10 YEARS
KATHRINE 9 YEARS
MAYA 11 YEARS
GRY 14 YEARS
HOLGER 7 YEARS
HOLGER 7 YEARS

Animals on the farm

Paul the Pig

Paul here doesn't quite resemble a real pig. His head is too big, but because his snout, small legs, ears, and the curl on his tail have a shape we associate with pigs, there is no doubt that he is still recognized as a pig.

1.

THE PIG HERE IS SEEN FROM A RIGHT SIDE ANGLE, SO HIS CHEEK PROTRUDES ON THE LEFT SIDE.

2.

3.

THE PIG'S LEGS ARE SHORT AND ANGULAR.

4.

THE PIG'S FACE IS LOCATED ON THE LOWER PART OF THE HEAD. THE EYES ARE SMALL, THE SNOUT IS OVAL, AND THE MOUTH IS WIDE AND NARROW.

YOUR LINE DRAWING IS PROBABLY BEAUTIFUL ON ITS OWN, BUT A PINK COLOR WILL DEFINITELY MAKE YOUR PIG LOOK LIKE A PIG.

Gavin the Goat

The goat has horns, a long face, a muzzle with broad, narrow nostrils, and drooping ears.

1.

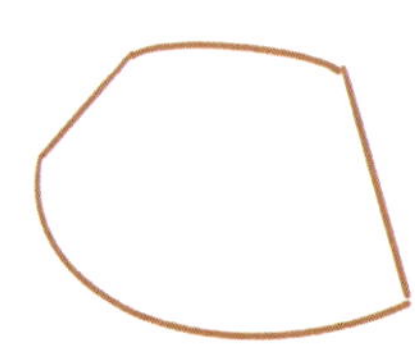

THE GOAT'S FACE IS DRAWN IN TWO PARTS. THE UPPER PART IS ANGULAR, AND THE LOWER PART IS ROUNDED.

2.

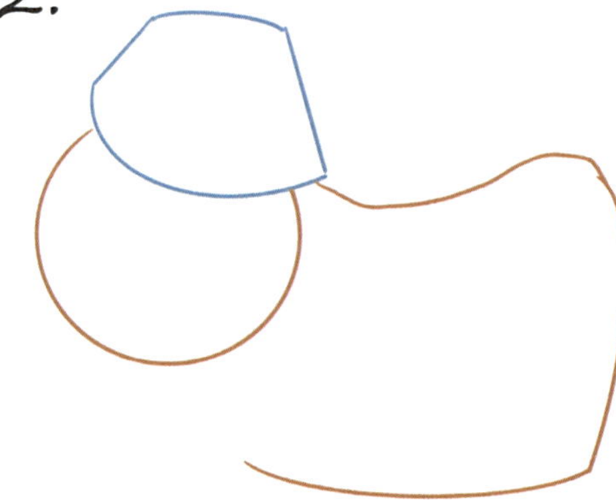

3.

BOTH THE EARS AND THE EYES ARE OVAL-SHAPED. MAKE BOTH SLIGHTLY LARGER ON THE GOATS LEFT SIDE.

4.

THE LEGS ARE SMALL SQUARE BLOCKS.

5.

THE MOUTH IS WIDE. IT STRETCHES ACROSS ALMOST THE ENTIRE MUZZLE AND IS CONNECTED TO THE NOSE WITH A GENTLY CURVED LINE.

6.

THE GOAT HERE APPEARS TO BE WHITE, BUT IT IS ACTUALLY COLORED WITH A LIGHT BLUE SHADE. WHAT COLOR WOULD YOU LIKE YOUR GOAT TO BE? PERHAPS IT COULD HAVE SPOTS.

Carla the Cow

The cow's head is elongated with a broad muzzle and large nostrils. It has small horns and a visible udder. And Carla here has spots, which are also characteristic of many cows.

1.

2.

THE COW'S BODY IS SQUARE, BUT LET THE LINES CURVE SLIGHTLY TO MAKE THE SHAPE MORE LIVELY.

3. THE NOSTRILS ARE SLIGHTLY OVAL AND ARE SITUATED WITH A SIGNIFICANT DISTANCE ON EACH SIDE OF THE MUZZLE.

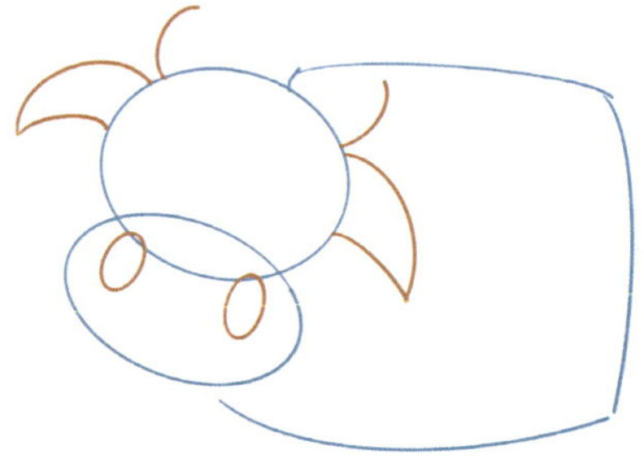

4.

THE TWO CURVES FROM THE MUZZLE UP TO EACH EAR INDICATE THAT THE COW'S HEAD IS THREE-DIMENSIONAL.

5.

THE COW DOES NOT NECESSARILY HAVE SPOTS. YOU CAN DECIDE WHETHER YOURS SHOULD HAVE THEM AND HOW THEY SHOULD BE POSITIONED. HOWEVER, CARLA HERE DOES HAVE SOME LARGE, LOVELY COW SPOTS.

Randy the Rooster

The rooster has a comb on its head and a large, beautiful tail. This one is a bit chubby, but you can choose to make yours slimmer if you prefer as long as you give him these characteristics.

1.

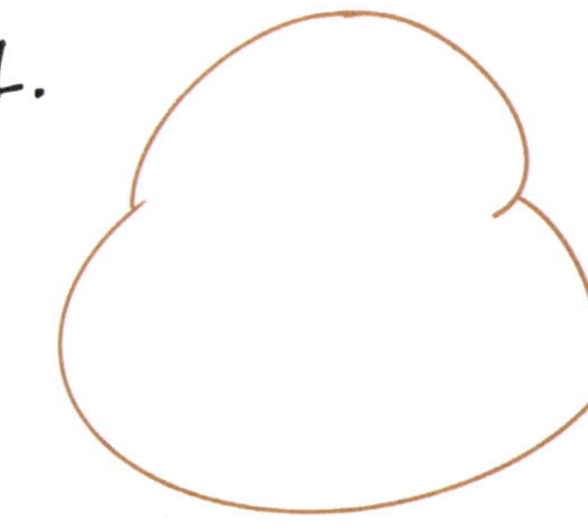

THE ROOSTER'S BODY DOESN'T NEED TO BE SHAPED EXACTLY LIKE THIS. THE MOST IMPORTANT ASPECT OF THE SHAPE IS THE SMALL NOTCH THAT SEPARATES THE HEAD FROM THE BODY.

2.

3.

THE ROOSTER'S THIGHS ARE MUSCULAR AND LARGE. THE HIND THIGH IS ALMOST HIDDEN BEHIND THE BODY.

4.

THE CURVE BETWEEN THE ROOSTER'S EYES IS THE BEGINNING OF THE BEAK. ON EACH SIDE, THE ROOSTER'S CHEEKS ARE MARKED WITH A CURVE THAT COVERS THE LOWER PART OF THE EYE.

5.

6. THE BOTTOM EDGE OF THE ROOSTER'S COMB IS DRAWN WITH AN S-SHAPED CURVE. A COUPLE OF CURVES FROM WHERE THE COMB MEETS THE HEAD INDICATE THAT IT IS FOLDED OUT TO THE SIDE LIKE A FANCY HAIRSTYLE.

7.

YOU CAN COLOR YOUR ROOSTER LIKE THIS ONE, OR YOU CAN GIVE HIM OTHER COLORS. FOR EXAMPLE, THE TAIL WOULD ALSO LOOK BEAUTIFUL IF IT HAD MULTIPLE DIFFERENT COLORS.

Susan the Sheep

The sheep is perhaps the simplest drawing in this book. A sheep is essentially just a big clump of wool with a protruding snout.

DRAW THE SHEEP'S BODY AS A SQUARE. LET THE LINES CURVE SLIGHTLY TO MAKE THE FIGURE MORE LIVELY.

THE EYES ARE OVAL-SHAPED, WITH THE FARTHEST ONE BEING SLIGHTLY SMALLER THAN THE FRONT ONE. THE NOSE IS A BROAD V SHAPE LOCATED JUST BELOW THE EYES.

4.

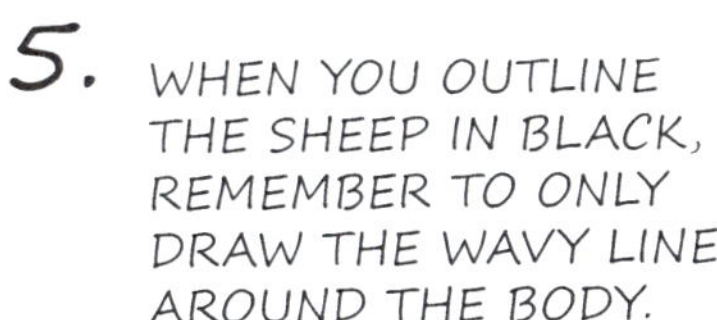

5. WHEN YOU OUTLINE THE SHEEP IN BLACK, REMEMBER TO ONLY DRAW THE WAVY LINE AROUND THE BODY.

” SUSAN IS SLIGHTLY PINK, BUT PERHAPS YOU SAW HIM AS WHITE. THE SAME APPLIES TO SHEEP IN NATURE, WE PERCEIVE THEM AS WHITE, BUT IN FACT, THEY HAVE A BIT OF COLOR (ALTHOUGH NOT PINK).

Children and parents draw Animals on the Farm

MAYA 6 YEARS

ASGER'S MOM 37 YEARS

ASGER 5 YEARS

GRY 14 YEARS

FENJA'S DAD 39 YEARS

FENJA 14 YEARS

MAYA 11 YEARS

LUCA 6 YEARS

Animals by the water

Bert the Beaver

The beaver has a large, broad tail. Bert's tail is actually so big that he can take a nap on it. And a beaver has large incisors that can gnaw through thick tree trunks.

1.

THE BEAVER'S BODY IS SHAPED LIKE AN EGG.

2.

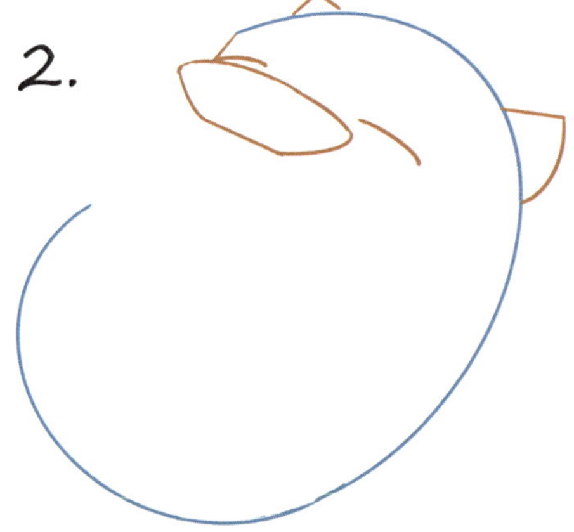

DRAW A BROAD NOSE. IT SHOULD BE ABOUT HALF AS WIDE AS THE BEAVER'S HEAD.

3.

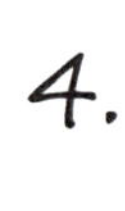

THE BEAVER'S TAIL EXTENDS FROM THE BOTTOM OF THE RUMP TO THE TOP OF THE HEAD. A LINE PARALLEL TO THE INSIDE OF THE TAIL MAKES IT APPEAR THICK AND FLUFFY.

5.

DRAW A CHECKERED PATTERN OVER THE BEAVER'S TAIL – LET THE LINES BREAK, FOLLOWING THE SHAPE OF THE TAIL ALONG THE EDGE.

6.

❞ THE EDGE OF THE BEAVER'S TAIL IS DARKER THAN THE UPWARD-FACING PART. THIS GIVES THE TAIL DEPTH.

Drew the Dragonfly

The dragonfly has a long, slender body, large eyes, and two sets of narrow wings. The tail is striped and curves slightly.

1.

THE DRAGONFLY'S HEAD IS AN OVAL SHAPE WITH AN OVAL ON EACH SIDE (THE EYES). ONLY A SMALL PART OF THE RIGHT EYE IS VISIBLE, THE REST IS HIDDEN BEHIND THE HEAD.

2.

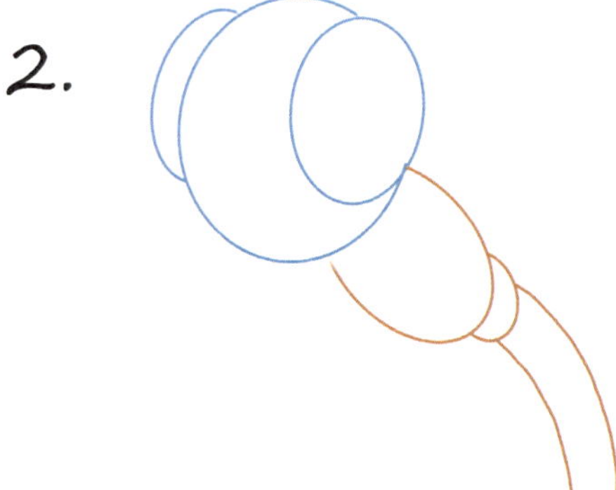

3.

THE WINGS ARE POSITIONED HIGH ON THE BACK, RIGHT BEHIND THE HEAD.

4.

5.
DRAW CURVED STRIPES DOWN THE DRAGONFLY'S TAIL TO MAKE IT APPEAR ROUNDED.
6.
THE REAR PART OF THE DRAGONFLY HAS A METALLIC SHEEN. YOU CAN ACHIEVE THE GLOSSY EFFECT BY ADDING A HIGHLIGHT ALONG THE TOP OF THE TAIL.

Frank the Frog

A frog has large, bulging eyes, a wide mouth, big thighs, and long toes with webbing in between.

1.

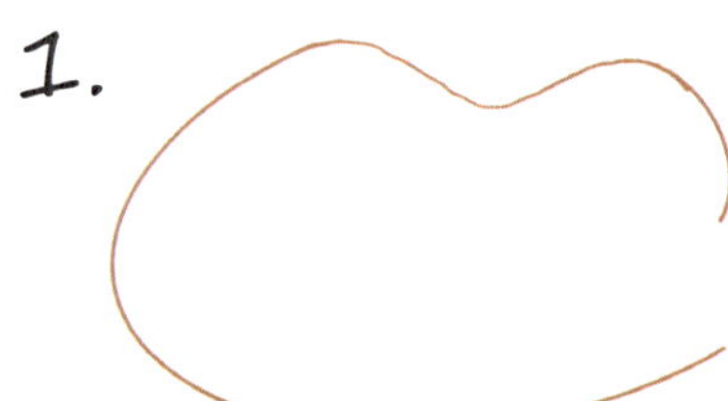

THE BEGINNING OF THE FROG'S HEAD AND BODY MAY LOOK COMPLICATED, BUT START BY DRAWING A TILTED C SHAPE. FROM THE TOP OF THE C, ADD AN S-SHAPED CURVE.

2.

3.

4.

DRAW THE FROG'S FEET IN THE SHAPE OF A KITE.

5.
FROM EACH CORNER OF THE FROG'S FEET,
DRAW A LINE POINTING TOWARDS THE LEG.
6.
AT THE END OF EACH LINE ON THE FROG'S FEET,
DRAW A SMALL CIRCLE.
7.
A FROG DOESN'T NECESSARILY
HAVE TO BE GREEN. YOU CAN TRY
USING A DIFFERENT COLOR, OR
EVEN ADD SOME SPOTS AROUND IT.

Olga the Otter

The otter is long and slender with a strong tail. It has small ears and a broad snout. And it has a characteristic ”muzzle” and whiskers.

1.

2.

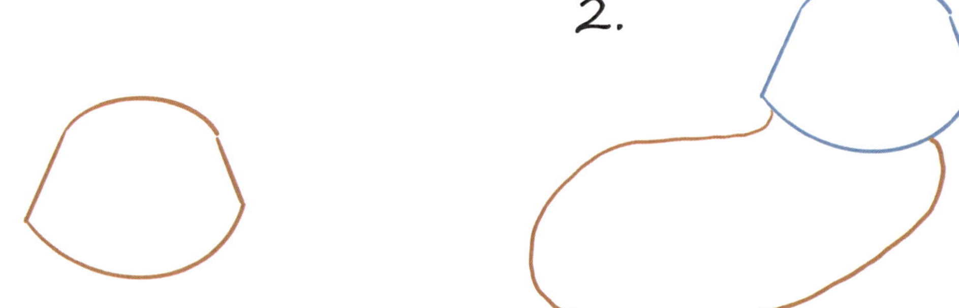

THE OTTER'S BACK GENTLY CURVES. THIS CAN BE REPRESENTED BY DRAWING THE BACK AS A FLAT S-SHAPE.

3.

THE EARS ARE SMALL AND LOCATED ON THE SIDES OF THE HEAD.

4.

5.
THE TAIL IS THICKEST CLOSEST TO THE BODY AND TAPERS TO A POINT AT THE END.
6.
7.
COLOR THE OTTER WITH BROWN TONES. USE THE LIGHTEST SHADE AT THE BOTTOM OF THE FACE AND ON THE BELLY.

Sophia the Swan

The swan is known for its beauty and elegance. It has a long, slender neck, large wings, and a distinctive black marking around the top of its beak and eyes.

1.

THE BODY IS SHAPED LIKE A LEAF, WITH THE POINTED END POINTING UPWARDS.

2.

DRAW A SHARP BEND IN THE WING, BUT NOTE THAT THE LINE STILL POINTS UPWARD.

3.

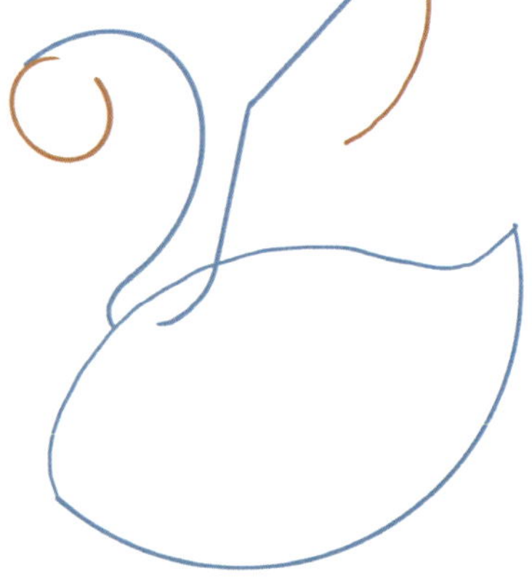

THE SWAN'S HEAD IS A SMALL CIRCLE AT THE END OF THE S-SHAPED NECK.

4.

5.

THE SWAN HERE APPEARS TO BE WHITE, BUT IN REALITY, IT IS COLORED WITH GRAY TONES. IN NATURE, WHITE IS RARELY PURE WHITE, AND EVEN IF SOMETHING IS WHITE, SHADOWS FALL UPON IT, MAKING THE COLOR DARKER.

Children and parents draw animals by the water

LUCA'S MOM 35 YEARS
KATHRINE 9 YEARS
ASGER 5 YEARS
ASGER 5 YEARS
FENJA 14 YEARS

For more inspiration, check this out...

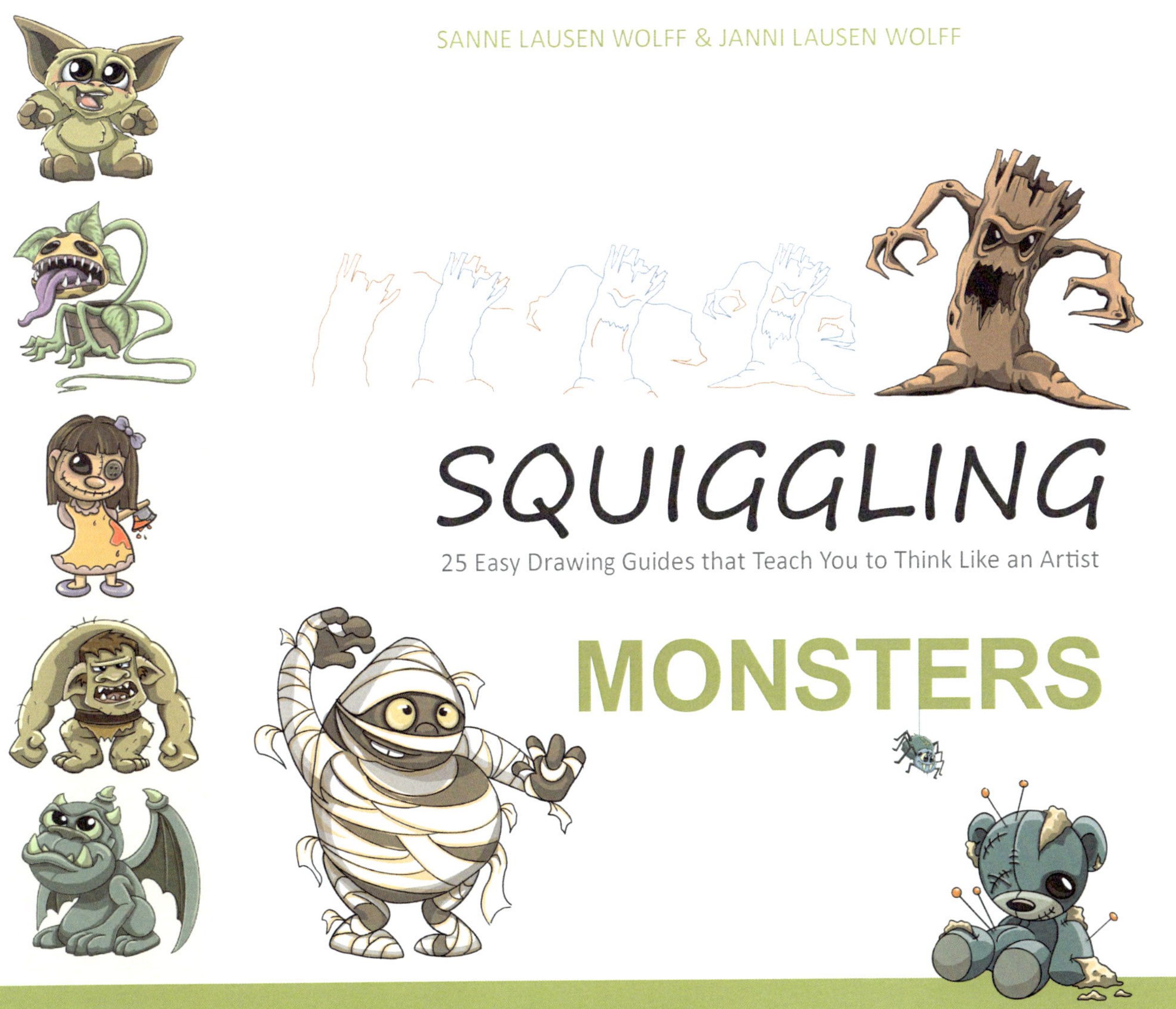

www.ingramcontent.com/pod-product-compliance
Ingram Content Group UK Ltd.
Pitfield, Milton Keynes, MK11 3LW, UK
UKRC032322290726
14090UKWH00005B/412

* 9 7 8 8 7 9 7 4 0 8 7 4 2 *